BENCH MARKS

by

Gil Burnett

Gil Burnett

2001

Illustrated by

Jay Melind

ISBN Number 0-9702857-0-1

Published by A Bench Press

Manufactured in the United States of America
    01 02 03 04   10 9 8 7 6 5 4 3 2 1

For Betsy, Sandra and Stephen who continually fill this father's heart with pride.

In memory of my father, John Henry Burnett, an attorney in whose footsteps I finally stopped resisting and followed.

BENCH MARKS

CONTENTS

ACKNOWLEDGMENTS

I would like to thank the many judges, lawyers, law enforcement officials, witnesses, and even defendants in criminal court for their contributions to this book.

Bob Rochelle, Charlie (Bubba) DeLuka, Susie Jones, and John J. Burney, Jr., are people I would especially like to thank for their interesting anecdotes. I also wish to thank Judges Leonard VanNoppen, Phil Ginn, Stanley Brown, Earl Fowler, Abner Alexander, Jim Hardison, and Grafton Beaman for their contributions.

My gratitude goes out to Barbara McChesney, Omar Mardan, and Julian Burnett for their helpful suggestions and encouragement.

This book never would have gotten off the ground without the assistance of Nancy Hanks Burnett. She spent many hours assisting in the selection of stories and correcting my grammar when I first began to write them down.

A special word of thanks goes to Don Trivette for his encouragement, and for introducing me to the computer. Without it, I might not have attempted *Bench Marks*.

When I was introduced to Jay Melind, and discovered just how talented he was, I couldn't imagine having anyone else illustrate my stories. Lucky for me, he agreed to do them.

Also, lucky for me, Rebecca Lewis agreed to edit this book. I turned over the manuscript to her, and she rewrote, retyped, reorganized, and rewarded me with a finished product that I could present to you. Her help was invaluable to me.

AUTHOR'S NOTE

When I was first seated on the District Court bench many years ago, a man telephoned me one day and said, "Judge, can I ask you a question?"

"Okay, what is it?"

"Would you please tell me," he continued, "what's the difference between fornication and adultery?"

"What?! You want to know the difference between fornication and adultery?" I asked somewhat surprised.

"That's right, Judge. You see," he continued after pausing for several seconds, "I've tried 'em both, and I don't see no difference!"

Well, when I hung up the phone and quit laughing, I decided to write down the conversation. That turned out to be the first of many anecdotes I collected while presiding as Chief Judge for the Fifth Judicial District of North Carolina.

When I first started doing this, I had no literary aspirations. I just wrote down what struck me as funny or interesting and dropped it in a drawer. As the years flowed by, it became a habit. I also gathered stories told to me by my contemporaries. By the time I retired, after 23 years on the bench, I had a drawer stuffed full of recollections.

The result turned out to be an informal collection of tales inside and outside of the courtroom, which I have organized into the book you now hold in your hands. I tried to gather the most humorous or interesting stories for you to read. Since miscreants are not an endangered species, I had to sift through a lot of raw material. As you read on, my hope is that I've provided you with a little entertainment and at least one chuckle, or maybe even two or three.

Incidentally, the names of most of the individuals involved in what you are about to read have either been omitted or changed to protect, mainly, the guilty!

KEEP A STRAIGHT FACE

Maintaining the proper decorum in my courtroom meant that I had to set an example by treating each case seriously, and with the focused, undivided attention that they all deserved. The following incidents illustrate why it was sometimes very difficult for me to keep a straight face . . . .

One morning a skinny little man stood before me, who apparently had an unusually heavy foot on the accelerator pedal of his battered old pick-up truck. Having been charged with speeding on numerous occasions, the fellow apparently felt an urgency to explain exactly how this could have possibly happened to him again.

Rotating his hat in his hands, he looked up at me and solemnly explained, "Judge, my separator just got stuck."

On another occasion, a young man appeared, charged with a DWI offense. Folks think that means "driving while impaired or intoxicated," which is correct, even though there is a more legally exacting definition. When officers stop people suspected of a

DWI, they routinely require them to perform field sobriety tests. One such test is the "gaze and nestagna" test which checks one's eyes for alcohol influenced impairment.

Having experienced this, the defendant tried to be helpful. He volunteered, "The officer gave me the 'gaze and stagger' test, Judge!"

Not long after that, another man stood up and explained that upon being suspected of a DWI on a country road late one night, a deputy sheriff had given him the "field variety test."

Another DWI case I heard included a scuffle which ensued when a state trooper had to wrestle a bald-headed man out of his pick-up truck. They both rolled into a ditch before the trooper managed to subdue him by spraying mace in his face.

Now standing meekly before me, with his shiny head bowed, the defendant solemnly muttered, "Judge, the officer seduced me with mace."

Sometimes after hearing cases like those described above, I'd have to recess court for fifteen minutes to regain my "proper decorum!"

BIG SAM

Throughout his eighty-nine years, Big Sam put in many appearances in my courtroom. He was a huge man with a good sense of humor which he never failed to bring with him into my courtroom. I saw a lot of him for what I call "mess." He simply got drunk and caused trouble.

On one occasion, his appearance before me reminded me of a game I played with my brother and sisters as a child. It was called "May I?" in which the player must ask permission to move. Big Sam had stolen an old coat from the Goodwill Industries Store. I asked him why in the world he'd stolen it knowing full well that, if he qualified, he probably could have gotten it for free. "Hell, they gonna give it away anyhow!" he complained in a loud, but jovial voice.

I patiently reminded him, "That's not the point. You didn't ask." I felt like ordering him to take two steps backwards, and ask "May I?"!!

Another time when Big Sam ran afoul of the law, he graced our courtroom with this good-natured complaint: "Judge, they sure has got a lotta laws nowadays," he sighed. "When I's born over close to

Lumberton, they didn't have no laws."

Maybe he was older than we thought!

ONE TO PLEAD, ONE TO PONDER

At a judges' conference, Judge Earl Fowler told me about this civil case he heard up in Asheville one day. He said the plaintiff, who had only one attorney representing him, noticed that the defendant had two lawyers. He sat quietly and watched as both of the defense attorneys would alternate arguing their client's case before Judge Fowler.

The trial went on for a while, and sometimes one of the defense attorneys would ask to "approach the bench." Judge Fowler would grant permission, whereupon the attorney would go up for a brief discussion, often leaving the other lawyer seated at the defense table.

After observing this for a while, the plaintiff grew concerned. He tugged at his lawyer's coat sleeve, and whispered, "He's got two lawyers, and I want two."

"Why?"

"Because," he replied, "when one of his lawyers is up there at the bench talkin' to the judge, the other one's sittin' over there thinkin'. But over here, when you're standin' up there talkin' to the judge, ain't nobody over here thinkin'!"

THE DOOR AND THE DEVIL

One day I looked up from the bench to see an unshackled, six-foot tall muscular prisoner, weighing approximately 200 pounds, being escorted into my courtroom by a bailiff for his first appearance. Dressed in an orange jail jumpsuit, he was there to be advised of the charges against him, his right to an attorney, bail bond, etc. When the bailiff placed him before the bench, the prisoner gave us not the slightest hint that he harbored an urgent desire to part company with us.

Now I should tell you that the courtroom is about ninety feet square. The judge sits behind the bench which is raised about a foot and a half off the floor. He or she can look straight ahead to the back of the courtroom where there are two very thick, solid oak doors which swing open to allow the public to enter. The aisle proceeds from the doors straight through the bar area to the bench. What most people do not realize, including the prisoner apparently, is that the right door, as you exit, is kept locked with a dead bolt. This is done just in case someone decides to run who shouldn't.

As I started to read the charges to him, the prisoner suddenly whirled around and took off like a rocket, dashing for the door, the right door. He flew right by the startled bailiff not realizing that he was about to encounter an immovable object, the *locked* right door.

Needless to say, when he hit that door, he "gave" and the door didn't! Blood splattered everywhere as the two collided with a loud wham! With no effort whatsoever, the door knocked the prisoner out cold, and he collapsed bleeding all over the courtroom aisle.

Bailiffs pounced on him immediately, and it wasn't long before the prisoner started "coming to." This time, three bailiffs escorted him up to the bench. As he stumbled forward, we all overheard him mumble, "The Devil made me do it."

JUST THE BARE FACTS

Maggie Jenkins, a voluptuous, twenty year-old bleached blond, was hauled into court for neglect of her infant daughter. She sat at the defense table swinging her crossed left leg while her court-appointed attorney questioned a witness in the case. Jordan Benning, a Protective Services' social worker was on the stand testifying.

"Have you interviewed Maggie Jenkins?" the attorney asked.

"Yes, I have," responded Ms. Benning.

"Well, did my client tell all? In other words, did she make a clean breast of it?"

I heard snickering throughout the courtroom. It turned out that the attorney and I were about the only people in the room who didn't know that Maggie was a topless dancer!

THE EYES HAVE IT

This courtroom story was related to me at one of many judges' conferences I attended throughout my years on the bench. I don't recall who shared it with me. Nevertheless, I hurriedly wrote it down and stuffed it in my "story drawer" back in 1975.

Mr. Johnson, a prosecution witness in an armed robbery case, leaned calmly back in the witness chair with his thumbs hooked around his colorful suspenders. He was being rigorously cross-examined by the defendant's lawyer. The lawyer was becoming exasperated with Mr. Johnson, who steadfastly maintained that he could see the defendant robbing the victim 50 yards away, even though it was in the middle of the night.

Raising his voice in frustration, the lawyer boomed, "Mr. Johnson, you really couldn't see what happened that far away on such a dark night, now could you?"

"Yes, I could," he insisted. "A street light lit up the area."

"But you were about fifty yards away. Correct?"

"Yes, sir. I reckon that's about right."

"Well now," the defendant's lawyer pointed out, "fifty yards is a long way to see at night. Explain to the court, please, how you could see what was going on at that distance, Mr. Johnson."

"I have good eyes."

"Oh, really? Well, since you have such good eyesight Mr. Johnson, please tell the jury just how far you can see at night, if you will."

Mr. Johnson thought for a few seconds. Then looking straight at the jury, he answered, "Well, on a clear night, I can see the moon." Then turning back toward the defense lawyer, he innocently asked, "How far is that?"

GET IT RIGHT!

Wayne, twelve, and Kevin, thirteen, skipped school one day, stole a motor scooter, and went joyriding. They were promptly caught red-handed by Officer Todd Lewis. Nevertheless, when their case came to trial, they both entered pleas of "not guilty," and denied knowing anything about it.

Officer Lewis took the stand and testified that he saw both boys riding on the motor scooter at the same time. As the boys listened intently, the officer was asked who was driving.

Glancing first at the two boys, the officer replied, "Wayne was driving, and Kevin rode on the back."

Both of the boys were so wrapped up in the testimony, that without thinking, they each jumped up and pointed to the other almost simultaneously.

Wayne was first to exclaim, "No! I was on the back. Kevin was drivin'."

"Yeah!" nodded Kevin in agreement. "I was drivin', and he rode on the back."

Officer Lewis smiled. Case closed.

THE AMERICAN WAY

A young father of three was on trial for non-support. Standing before me, he pulled his wallet out of his back hip pocket, and offered up plastic.

"Judge Burnett, I got $2,500 equity in my Master Card," he announced as he waved his credit card in the air.

Not understanding, I leaned forward and asked, "Would you please explain exactly what you mean?"

"Well, your Honor, I have a $5,000 limit on my Master Card, and I've only used $2,500. That means I got $2,500 equity left. You do take credit cards, don't you?"

BANTU x 5

My sister Susie, who lives in Raleigh, was cited to court for letting Bantu, her black Labrador retriever, run loose. She's a pretty sharp lady, so I was not surprised when she decided to plead her own case rather than hire a lawyer. Here are the facts, as they were related to me, that came out in court.

The whole thing started when a man, riding on a motorcycle with his wife on the back, pulled up and stopped at the intersection next to Susie's house. Revving his engine caused the surrounding neighbors' dogs to rev up their vocal cords in response. Some of them approached the biker couple barking furiously. The wife, deathly afraid of dogs, became frightened. She and her husband started kicking at the dogs, and one of them grabbed the man's leg.

When that happened, he panicked and started yelling, "I'm a hemophiliac! Help! I'm bleedin'!" before he even looked down to see if he'd been bitten. When he did look, he realized that there wasn't even a tear in his black leather pant's leg.

Susie came out to see what the commotion was all about, so the motorcyclist directed his anger toward her and her dog. The only trouble was, four of Susie's neighbors had black labs that were almost identical to Bantu. Since Susie maintained that her black lab was in her yard when she came outside, she pleaded not guilty, and the matter went to trial.

The operator of the motorcycle took the witness stand and testified.

On cross-examination, Susie asked the man, "Were there several black Labrador retrievers in the area?"

"Yes."

"Well, Sir," she continued, "would you say there was a total of five black labs?"

"Could have been."

"Is that a 'yes' or a 'no'?" Susie was enjoying herself.

"Yes," the man replied.

"Were some of them in the intersection, and some in my yard?"

"Yes," he admitted.

Then Susie moved in for the kill. "If the five Labrador retrievers were placed in a line-up, would you be able to identify which one bit you?"

The poor man hesitated for a minute, and then grudgingly admitted, "No, I guess not."

Susie turned to the judge and asked for a dismissal. She got it.

A CARPENTER, NOT A LAWYER

Judge Stanley Brown told me of a case he had in the Charlotte criminal court. Charlotte's the county seat of Mecklenburg County. The district attorney called the case, and the defendant, a tall skinny man, stepped forward. Dressed in a flowing robe, he looked like a hold-over flower child from the 1960's with his long hair and beard.

Judge Brown asked him if he would like to be represented by an attorney.

"Yes, your Honor, I wish to be represented by that greatest advocate of all time, Jesus Christ of Nazareth," he announced with a flourish.

Well, this request got the attention of everybody in the courtroom. All heads turned toward Judge Brown. The judge considered for a moment before replying, "Well, now that's a noble request, but I don't believe the Lord Jesus is licensed to practice law in Mecklenburg County. So would you like to be represented by someone who is?"

The colorfully attired defendant mulled this over for a minute before replying, "Yes, I believe I would."

So Judge Brown appointed him an earthly lawyer, not a carpenter.

WRONG COLORED S.O.B.

Judge Fleetwood was hearing a case in which a white man was being tried for assault. He had cut another white man with a knife in a heated argument.

Judge Fleetwood asked the defendant, "Why did you cut him?"

"Judge, he called me a white son-of-a-bitch."

"Even if he called you that," admonished Judge Fleetwood, "you still shouldn't have cut him."

"But, Judge, if he called you a white son-of-a-bitch, wouldn't you cut him?"

"Well, I'm not white, so it's not applicable," Judge Fleetwood pointed out.

"But Judge," the defendant persisted, "suppose he called you the kind of son-of-a-bitch you are?"

NICE TRY, ANYWAY

I remember one cold winter morning when the defendant in a case rolled into my courtroom in a wheelchair. He was a small man with a blanket draped across his lap, looking very contrite. After he'd been convicted of stealing, his lawyer, Mitch Perry, with a flair for the dramatic, practically cried trying to convince me to go easy "on this poor man *in a wheelchair.*"

Since he kept bringing it up, I asked Mr. Perry, "How was your client injured, causing him to wind up in a wheelchair?"

Sidestepping, Mr. Perry replied, "He's pitiful, Judge Burnett. He can't walk."

Again I asked, "How did he wind up in a wheelchair?"

Ignoring my question, Mr. Perry practically wailed, "Judge, as I said, he can't walk. He's confined to his bed or the wheelchair all the time."

I took a deep breath, and asked one more time, slowly and deliberately, "What happened to cause him to end up in a wheelchair?"

Realizing that he wasn't evoking my sympathy, Mr. Perry finally admitted, "Well, your Honor, he, uh . .

was shot and paralyzed while robbing a bank."

About two weeks later, I was telling this to another judge, and he shared a similar case with me. He said he listened to an attorney plead his guts out for a client portrayed as a "poor young orphan. She's alone in this cruel world. She has no one to turn to. She has no one to love her. She has no parents."

Apparently, this particular lawyer was one of those lawyers who just didn't know when to quit. The girl was orphaned because she had shot and killed both of her parents.

DREAM COME TRUE

A law enforcement officer assured me the following story actually happened in a South Carolina courtroom. Apparently by the time it reached me, it was one well-traveled tale. But just in case you haven't heard it, here it is.

A dignified, elderly lady had a twenty-year-old punk arrested and charged with "assault and attempted rape." When the case came to trial, the fragile little lady took the stand right after a lunch break. The judge was seated to her immediate right, and the jury sat several feet away to her left. Standing before her, the district attorney carefully led her through some preliminary questions.

Then he asked gently, "Now, Mrs. Bowden, please tell the jury exactly what happened."

She pointed a shaky finger toward the defendant, and timidly responded, "That young man sitting right there came up behind me and put his arms around me."

"How do you know it was the defendant?" asked the district attorney.

"Well, when he turned me around, I saw his face

very clearly."

"Thank you. Now did he say anything to you?"

Very uncomfortable, Mrs. Bowden replied, "Yes, he asked me if, if . . . . um, he said 'Would you like to, to . . . . ?' I cannot say that word."

The district attorney stepped closer to her, and said, "Ma'am, please just go ahead and tell the jury exactly what he said. It's okay."

Again she tried. "Well, he put his arms around me and asked, 'Would you like to . . . .?' " She paused, and pleaded with the judge, "Your Honor, I just cannot say that word."

The judge smiled gently at her and directed her to write down what the defendant had said to her. "Then we'll pass it over to the jury and let each one of them read it."

"Thank you, your Honor," she replied with relief. "I'll be glad to do that."

After writing down the question that the defendant had allegedly asked, she handed the note to the DA. He gave it to the juror seated in seat No. 1, who was instructed to read it and pass it down the line.

The juror in seat No. 4, a very attractive young lady, read it and tried to pass it on to juror No. 5. But juror No. 5 was an elderly gentleman who had nodded off. Apparently, he had not let jury duty interrupt his afternoon naptime. So the lovely juror No. 4 poked juror No. 5 with her finger, woke him up, and handed him the note. He read it, smiled at her, and tucked it in his coat pocket.

Surprised, the judge, who hadn't noticed that the gentleman juror was catnapping, said, "Sir, please pass that on so the other jurors might read it."

Startled, juror No. 5 exclaimed, "But, your Honor, this is sorta personal!"

BI-LINGUAL

One record-hot August, I had a man in court on trial for assault. He took the stand in his own defense and explained that an argument with his girlfriend had turned violent, and he blamed it first on the heat wave.

He said the heat had caused his girl friend's nerves to fray. Then he tried to justify his violent reaction to the verbal abuse that had rained down on his head, and had set him off. "Judge," he explained in a very indignant voice, "she was usin' her French. You know -- jawin'. We calls it Pig Latin. I'm tellin' you, she was cussin' at me like hell! I had to protect myself from that awful language!"

JACK ATTACK

For most of my career on the bench, many of my mornings began with breakfast at Whitey's Restaurant on Market Street. I enjoyed the fellowship that came with being one of the "regulars," and often times I'd sit and trade stories with my companions. One morning, I recounted this one that I had recently heard. It seemed appropriate considering what two of my fellow diners were eating.

A rather rotund man, defending himself against a DWI charge, took the stand in my courtroom one day. He was trying to place the blame everywhere except on his shoulders. During the course of his self-serving testimony, he even whined about the officer who arrested him.

Shifting his large frame around in the witness chair to face me, he informed me quite seriously, "Judge, Officer John William hit me on the head with his Flap Jack!"

YOU GIVE ME FEVER

One afternoon a state trooper took the stand to testify in a DWI case. The defendant, a middle-aged man, had been stopped when he was spotted weaving all over the highway. When the trooper had completed his testimony, the defendant took the stand in his own defense.

When his attorney asked him to explain the charge, he said, "I was sick. I had the black and white fever."

I said, "What kind of fever did you say?"

"I had the black and white fever, your Honor."

"Would you please explain to the Court just what kind of fever that is?"

"Yes, sir. You see," he explained earnestly, "when I saw that black and white patrol car in my rearview mirror, it made me sick. I got the black and white fever sure 'nuff. That's why I was drivin' all over the road."

THE HUNGARIAN HOBO

I'll never forget Mr. Szarek. His case was one of the saddest I ever heard. Originally from what used to be known as Hungary, his life had taken a downward spiral by the time he appeared before me in court charged with arson and public drunkenness.

He first came to the attention of Deputy Sheriff Julian who followed up on a report that some tourists had actually observed a middle-aged man eating the carcass of a porpoise which had washed up on the beach at Fort Fisher. Fort Fisher is at the southernmost tip of New Hanover County between the Cape Fear River and the Atlantic Ocean. Apparently, the homeless Mr. Szarek was living down there. The tourists and Deputy Julian gave him some food and cigarettes. Then the deputy contacted a minister who took Mr. Szarek to his parsonage, and gave him ten dollars in cash.

Interrupted by a call to come over to his church, the minister told Mr. Szarek, who was sitting in his kitchen, that he would be back shortly. Unfortunately, Mr. Szarek took off down the street, bought a bottle of Roma Rocket wine which he took back to the parsonage, and drank immediately. Then, he lit a cigarette and accidentally caught the parsonage on fire. Stumbling out into the street to escape his first transgression, he committed his second, being drunk in public. The next thing he knew, he had been hauled over from jail and was standing before me in court very subdued.

The minister was present, and stated that he felt somewhat responsible by leaving Mr. Szarek alone longer than he had intended. "Besides," he pointed out, "there wasn't much damage from the fire." Therefore, he asked the district attorney to dismiss the arson charge.

Then I asked Mr. Szarek, "What would you do if the public drunkenness charge against you was dismissed, and you could walk out of here a free man?"

He pulled himself up with as much dignity as he could muster and replied, "Your Honor, I vud leev Vilmington. I get too much help here. I don't vant de help. I vant to get out of town."

"Where would you go?" I asked.

"I vud go sout," he replied.

"South?"

"Yes, sout. I vant to leev here," he assured me.

So the D.A. and I conferred, and the D.A.

dismissed both charges against him. I directed Deputy Julian to take him back to jail and give him lunch before releasing him. I also slipped him some money to buy Mr. Szarek a little food for his trip. The deputy kicked in a few bucks, too.

At home that evening, I turned on the television in time to see Mr. Szarek on the 6:00 o'clock news waving good-bye to our city, clutching a Pepsi and a brown paper bag of goodies. The Cape Fear River Bridge could be seen in the background. I silently wished him well as he prepared to hitchhike his way "sout."

Unfortunately, we didn't have to wonder for long whatever happened to the poor man. About two weeks later, Deputy Julian stopped me one day in the courthouse hallway with this sad postscript. "Judge, when the Hungarian left town, I stuck my business card in his shirt pocket, and told him to call me if he ever needed help. I got a call from a man this morning who found the card."

"Not good, eh?"

"No, sir, he made it to a little town in Georgia where he died. I was told that he was hit and killed by a motorist while ridin' a bicycle on a highway late last night."

I sighed. "Well, we tried."

"Yeah, we did," he replied quietly. Then Deputy Julian shook his head and walked away.

COURTROOM DIAGNOSIS

One afternoon, a very attractive red-headed nurse stood before me charged with a DWI. She was quite tall. I'd guess at least six feet. After pleading guilty and being sentenced, she continued to stand there in front of the bench looking at me.

"Ma'am, you're free to go, now," I told her.

Instead of leaving, she asked very softly, "Your Honor, may I come closer to the bench?"

Curious, I said, "Yes."

She approached and leaned over the top toward me, cupped her right hand to the side of her mouth, and whispered, "Judge, you have granulated eyelids. You should get them checked by a physician."

Taking her advice, I did get my eyes checked. And sure enough, I had granulated eyelids!

EAR TODAY AND GONE TOMORROW

Here's a favorite case of law students. It happened in court long before Mike Tyson punched and chomped his way into infamy.

A burly defendant was charged with biting a man's ear off in a sidewalk brawl. His attorney, Mr. Spearman, had entered a plea of "not guilty," on his behalf. The victim, Pete Brinkley, had a witness to the altercation, Wilford Barney, who was being rigorously cross-examined by the defense attorney.

"Now, Mr. Barney, did you actually see my client bite Mr. Brinkley's ear off?"

"No, sir, I didn't."

"You didn't actually see my client bite off his ear? Is that your testimony?" repeated Mr. Spearman.

"That's my testimony," replied Mr. Barney. "I said I didn't."

Pleased with the response, Mr. Spearman turned and looked at the jury. Then he pushed his luck just a little too far. In a loud voice, he boomed, "Speak up now, Mr. Barney. For the benefit of the jury, would you state once again whether or not you *actually saw* my client bite off Pete Brinkley's ear?"

Mr. Barney paused for a moment, and then responded slowly and in the louder voice Mr. Spearman had requested, "As I've stated before," he replied testily, "I didn't *actually see* your client bite Pete's ear off. But I sure as hell did *actually see* him spit it out!"

THIS DOESN'T COUNT, DOES IT?

A well dressed young man, charged with his second DWI offense, appeared before me in court. He had been stopped while driving to his girlfriend's apartment across town. Since his license had been previously revoked, I asked him why he was driving a car.

Trying to be helpful, he obliged me with this explanation. "I was takin' the car to her house. You see, I needed to get her to drive me to the Clerk of Court's office, so I could try to get my driver's license back!"

Oh. . . .

(UN)LAWFUL LEEWAY

A highway patrolman went by the chambers of a friend of mine who's a judge in another state. He explained that he had stopped a motorist for speeding, but did not issue a citation.

"Why not? What happened?" asked the judge.

"Well, sir," laughed the officer, "I was on routine patrol in a 55 mile per hour zone, and I fell behind a man who was doin' about 50 miles an hour. I noticed that he looked at me through his rear-view mirror, and I guess he recognized my patrol car. But he speeded up, of all things. I couldn't believe it! He got up to around 65-70 mph, so I pulled him over."

"He actually speeded up when he saw you?"

"Yes, he did, and when I approached him, and told him he was speedin', he admitted it right off the bat!"

Imitating the motorist, the officer then related his story. "I know I was speeding, Officer, but when I saw you I panicked. Please let me explain," he hurried on. "Believe it or not, Officer, last week my wife ran off with a highway patrolman, and when I saw your patrol car behind me, I panicked. I thought you were bringing her back!"

The officer slapped his hand on his thigh, and laughed. "Judge, that's one of the most creative excuses I've ever heard. I just couldn't give him a ticket!"

WILL THE REAL JOHN DOE PLEASE STAND

Routinely in criminal court, I would occasionally see the name of the accused defendant written as "John Doe" ("Jane Doe" if female). This name was used when the authorities did not know the person's real name. If a male, it usually meant the accused was so drunk when he was arrested, that he couldn't give his name and probably didn't have any identification.

Sometimes, he'd just refuse to give his name, so for processing purposes he was temporarily designated as "John Doe." By the time he showed up in court, sobriety had kicked in, and he usually volunteered his correct name.

On one particular occasion, I routinely asked just such a defendant to state his name for the record.

He responded, "John Doe."

"No, I mean what is your *real* name? What name were you given at birth?" I asked.

"John Doe," he insisted.

"Your real name is John Doe?" I asked incredulously.

With a sigh that indicated he had been through this scenario many times before, he assured me that it was.

As I was driving home that night, I suddenly smiled and said to myself, "Yes, Virginia, there really is a John Doe!"

THE VOODOOING DEFENDANT

I had just given what's called a "first appearance" to this 5'11", 145 pound man who was charged with breaking and entering an empty house. He did no damage, but since he had a pretty bad track record for showing up in court when he was supposed to, I called for a bail bond. I also ordered a psychiatric evaluation, because I suspected that he had mental problems. What happened next confirmed my suspicions.

When the business of his first appearance was concluded, a bailiff escorted the man over to the prisoners' box to be seated while awaiting his return to jail. This is an area to the left of the judge's bench reserved specifically for prisoners. Then I quickly focused on the next case.

Suddenly, I heard a loud "hiss" coming from the prisoners' box. It sounded just like a large snake. Startled, I looked around and saw the prisoner who had just been seated, standing with his arms stretched straight out toward me, hissing away at me. His dark, bony fingers wiggled and vibrated, as one hiss after another spewed from his lips. Loud and long. Nonstop. This situation called for Dr. Bell, and I asked the bailiff to go and get him immediately. Now Dr. Bell isn't a real medical doctor. He's the liaison between the Mental Health Center and the Court, so we all call him "Doctor" Bell. Since his office was conveniently located just across the hall from the back of the courtroom, he arrived right in the middle of this high-dose hex session of which I was the increasingly uncomfortable target.

At the same time, the prisoner's sister, who was also present in the courtroom, came running down to the front shouting, "Judge, he ain't right! He ain't right!"

I knew she wasn't commenting on his transgressions. She, too, it seemed, felt that he had mental problems. Meanwhile, the hissing continued.

I asked Dr. Bell to call the Mental Health Center, and arrange for someone to come over and examine the man. I confided, "Tell 'em to hurry. He's puttin' a hex on me, and I think it's workin'!" I had goose bumps, and I could feel the hair on the back of my neck standing at attention.

Soon the poor man was led away still furiously hissing at me. The courtroom settled back down, and I continued on with the rest of the docket. But for the rest of the day, I had a funny feeling in the pit of my stomach. And I don't think it was the chili I ate for lunch, either.

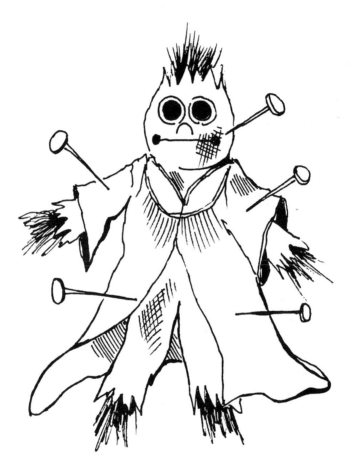

DUBIOUS DISTINCTION

Judge Abner Alexander told me about a case he heard one day in domestic criminal court up in Winston-Salem. The defendant who stood before him, a young man in his twenties, was asked if he was pleading "guilty" or "not guilty" to non-support of an out-of-wedlock child.

Hesitating, the defendant finally replied, "I plead not guilty and guilty, Judge."

Ab looked at him for a minute, and then acknowledged, "I haven't heard many pleas like that. What exactly do you mean?"

"Well, your Honor," continued the young man, "it's like this. Me and my buddy were both havin' sex with that girl, and we don't know which one of us knocked her up. So we talked it over and decided we'd both chip in on this thing."

"Oh, really? Well, that's interesting, but that's not the way it works. . . . No, I tell you what," Ab continued, "this is what you're going to do. I'm ordering you to take a blood test to determine paternity, and if it's negative, you pass. Then your buddy has to take one. But one of you is going to support this baby *until she reaches the age of eighteen.*"

The defendant appeared visibly shaken. He swallowed hard, nodded, and spoke no more.

GENEROUS JUDGE

One day, Jim Bowden, a courtly attorney affectionately known as "Mr. Jim," was representing one of his neighbors, a young man charged with non-support of his ex-wife. Judge Crutchfield was hearing the case.

Mr. Jim knew that his client didn't make much money, so he pleaded and pleaded with the judge not to require the man to pay much, if anything at all.

Finally weary of listening to Mr. Jim expound on his client's pauper-like condition, Judge Crutchfield looked at the defendant and said, "Young man, I've made up my mind. I'm going to give your wife $20 per week."

Mr. Jim's client brightened immediately. "Judge, that's great! Why, I'll kick in $10 myself!"

IT'S BEGINNING TO LOOK A LOT LIKE CHRISTMAS

When I sat on the bench, I could always tell when Christmas was getting closer. The weather usually turned cold enough to make you consider heading even farther south than we already are. North of town, the Kings Grant subdivision lit up like Las Vegas. The Salvation Army bell ringers stood patiently tending their kettles outside the downtown post office, and shoplifters hit the stores right and left. More than any other month of the year, December seemed to stimulate some people of all ages to steal something from a store. The ones who were caught showed up before me usually by mid-January.

1986 was no exception. A short, pudgy, middle-aged man stood accused of making numerous selections at a major department store without bothering to pay for any of them.

"Why did you steal these items?" I asked.

"I needed money, Judge Burnett."

"You needed money?"

"Yes, sir. First I was gonna sell the stuff to get money to buy presents for all my nieces and nephews for Christmas," he patiently explained.

"Oh, so you planned to sell what you stole?"

"Yes, sir. Then I decided to just give the stuff to them as presents. But," he reported indignantly, "they didn't like any of the things I stole!"

Imagine that . . . .

SPIRIT-ED INTERVENTION

There is a legend surrounding the Battleship USS North Carolina, permanently berthed across the Cape Fear River from downtown Wilmington. Nicknamed the "Showboat" by New Yorkers back in 1941 who watched her trips in and out of the New York Navy Yard while undergoing her shake-down cruises, she is purported to be inhabited by a ghost. One day I heard a case involving larceny by a work-release prisoner assigned to the Showboat. It fueled the rumor of a resident ghost onboard.

Since the battleship is a popular tourist attraction open year-round to the public, one of the duties of the assistant superintendent is to make routine security checks. But as the assistant superintendent, Mr. Schutt, took the stand to describe what happened on one of those security checks, you will see that it was anything but "routine."

After being sworn in, Mr. Schutt proceeded to relate how he made his rounds, aided by a flashlight, in order to inspect those darkened areas of the ship which are routinely excluded from public viewing. In those off-limit areas, all of the bulkhead doors are kept locked, he explained, and all light bulbs and door knobs, as well as their shafts, had been removed. This included the bilge, and most of the lower sections of the Showboat, both fore and aft, he pointed out.

On the particular day in question, Mr. Schutt had descended several decks, when his flashlight beam illuminated a wheel on one of the bulkhead scuttle hatches. Suddenly he froze. The wheel, which had been shackled to a post by a heavy chain secured with a padlock, was moving! It turned slowly -- first clockwise, and then counterclockwise. Mr. Schutt, who said he'd never believed in ghosts, started reconsidering his position.

He clambered back up the ladders to get his supervisor. As the two men descended once again to the old wheel, the assistant superintendent related to his boss what he had seen. This time, the wheel was deathly still. But upon closer inspection, the flashlight beam revealed the chain had been cut. So the two men decided to inspect the other side of the bulkhead. Unlocking the padlock, Mr. Schutt turned the wheel counterclockwise to unlock the scuttle hatch. Then they pulled open the door and stepped into the next compartment. The beam of the flashlight sliced through the blackness revealing nothing. Not a soul was there, earthly or otherwise.

Nevertheless, they continued their inspection, by unlocking the hatch on the far side of the compartment, and proceeding forward toward the bow of the battleship. Next, Mr. Schutt described how they systematically started up ladders checking each deck in that area.

Finally, several decks above the old wheel, the powerful beam of the flashlight revealed a man huddled in a far corner of one compartment. Mr. Schutt said he recognized the man as one of the prisoners present that day on work release. When he was asked if he had been down below, the prisoner said, "No." Asked if he'd seen anyone else in the area, he replied that he hadn't.

Still puzzled, the assistant superintendent and his boss proceeded through another hatch, and spotted a second prisoner crouched in a darkened corner. This one, Mr. Schutt testified, clutched a flashlight and a doorknob with its shaft attached.

The second prisoner, charged with larceny of those items, steadfastly maintained that he had not been any farther below deck than where he was discovered. Even though he appeared to be guilty, the case was dismissed on a technicality. Nevertheless, he was removed from the work release program.

But to this day, I still wonder who or what turned that wheel. And would those two prisoners have been found so promptly without a little spirit-ed intervention? Your guess is as good as mine.

INTERNAL COMBUSTION

Judge Grafton Beaman told me of a case he heard in which a man was charged with making a false fire alarm report.

The fire department, after swiftly dispatching two trucks in response to an urgent call, discovered it was a false alarm. So the tape of the call was turned over to law enforcement authorities. The voice on the tape was recognized as a man who was well known as a habitual drunk.

After he was arrested, he stood before Judge Beaman and pled guilty as charged. The judge scolded him for wasting taxpayers' money and possibly jeopardizing lives unnecessarily by reporting a fire when there wasn't one.

"But Judge," the defendant protested, "there really was a fire. I gotta holt of some bad liquor, and I was burnin' up inside!"

ROAD RAGE SOUTHERN STYLE

This is a sad case, because it could so easily have been avoided. It involved a young man from out-of-state driving his brand new, red Mercedes convertible and a young man from New Hanover County driving an old Ford pick-up truck. The boy in the truck had a buddy riding with him.

According to the evidence presented in court, the driver of the Mercedes convertible was headed north on Market Street, when he started making a right turn. Realizing he was at the wrong intersection, he abruptly whipped back onto Market Street causing the driver of the pick-up truck, who was right behind him, to swerve left to avoid an accident.

"Watch where you're goin'!" shouted the truck driver angrily, as he stomped down on the gas and came up to the driver's side of the Mercedes.

In response, the sports car driver made an obscene gesture with the middle finger of his left hand. That's when the trouble really started. The pick-up truck driver let the Mercedes get back in front of him, and then he rammed the convertible in the rear. As the Mercedes bounced forward, the driver figured the best thing for him to do would be to leave the old pick-up in his dust. He gunned his engine, and pulled away from the truck. But the truck driver had "snapped," and he put the pedal to the metal. The chase was on.

The truck rammed the sports car again and again. Testimony in court revealed that both vehicles exceeded 100 miles per hour. Since the old truck was keeping up with the Mercedes, the driver decided to try something different. He turned into a pasture, hoping to out-maneuver his pursuer. But the truck flew into the pasture, too, and headed straight for the Mercedes. When the battered sports car swerved to avoid a fence, the truck driver plowed right into it on the driver's side. It crushed the sports car, and sent its young owner to the hospital, seriously injured.

The hapless victim recovered, and took the witness stand admitting ruefully, "Judge, it's been an expensive lesson."

The driver of the Ford pick-up truck grudgingly admitted that he shouldn't have assaulted the man. The judge hoped that just maybe the truck driver had learned a lesson, too. That hope was quickly shattered however, when the young man shrugged his shoulders and whined, "But, Your Honor, when he gave me the finger, it just made me mad!"

So?

DEPRIVED

As a trial judge, having your life threatened is an occupational hazard. I received my share of threats over the years, and they were always treated seriously. My family and I received protective security on these occasions, until the matters were resolved.

Shortly before I retired, I arrived at the courthouse one Friday morning to find a crowd of employees standing outside. A deputy quickly informed me that a man, sounding very knowledgeable about explosives, had called the sheriff and a radio station several times stating that he had placed a bomb in the courthouse to kill me. But concern for the safety of others in the building prompted him to place calls to warn them to get out first. On one of his calls, he was stupid enough to talk on the phone long enough for the call to be traced. Consequently, he was quickly arrested, and things around the courthouse settled back to normal.

The following Tuesday morning, shortly after court was opened, the bailiff came up to the bench and whispered, "Judge Burnett, the man who threatened to kill you is coming into court from jail in a few minutes for his first appearance before you."

Well I knew that it would be highly improper for me to get involved in the man's case. Since he had allegedly threatened to blow me to smithereens, I might be slightly prejudiced! But I just couldn't resist having a little word with him first.

When the defendant was brought forward to stand before me, I said very seriously, "According to this warrant, it looks like you wanted to do me harm."

He stood in front of the bench, looking at the floor, and shook his head furiously from side to side.

So I tried again. "I understand that you said you put a bomb in the courthouse."

Still gazing at the floor, he again shook his head negatively.

"Since your charges indicate a threat toward me, I suppose I should not hear your case," I stated.

The man stopped staring at the floor, looked up at me, and started vigorously shaking his head up and down in agreement with me. I could not help but be amused. "Take the defendant to courtroom 301," I told the bailiff, "and let the judge over there give him his first appearance."

As the man was led out of the courtroom, he looked extremely relieved. I never saw him again. Later on, a deputy told me that the guy was angry with

me   because I   had   locked up his girlfriend in jail.
Apparently, he missed her. . . .

DEGREED DEFENDANT

A motorist from New York was speeding south on U.S. Highway 17, when a state trooper pulled him over and issued him a "courtesy citation." (A courtesy citation is a ticket which does not require bail bond nor incarceration, but is issued with the expectation that the defendant will appear in court at a later date. Isn't that a nice name for a ticket?!) In this case, the motorist decided to go immediately to the courthouse to see if the matter could be resolved. That would save him from having to come back later.

Court was in session, and the man approached the district attorney. The judge overheard him informing the DA, in no uncertain terms, that he knew his rights and that he was not doing 75 mph in a 55 mph zone, as charged. He further stated that he had a bachelor of science degree, and was working on his master's degree. He even pointed out that he had had a course in law. The implication he wished to convey was that of a very well-educated man.

The ticketing officer was not present in court. Nevertheless, to help the defendant since he did admit that he *might* have been going "a little over 55 mph," the district attorney agreed to let him plead guilty to exceeding the posted speed limit. The motorist accepted this and left to pay his fine.

As the New Yorker strode from the courtroom, the judge was overheard muttering under his breath, "That man seems to be educated beyond his intelligence."

I PICKED FLOWERS

The defendant, who was charged with several misdemeanors, had talked with Attorney James Flowers about representing him in court. For the man's first appearance, however, Mr. Flowers was not present.

Not knowing the accused had hired a lawyer, the judge asked, "Sir, would you like the court to appoint you an attorney?"

"No, Judge, I don't need no lawyer. I'm gonna use Mr. Flowers."

DRIVING, FLYING -- WHAT'S THE DIFFERENCE?

Before court, I sat down for breakfast at my usual table. Swapping yarns, smoking cigarettes, eating eggs, grits and bacon, drinking coffee, and offering up advice on solving the world's problems was already in full swing when I got there.

Bob Rochelle, retired from Southern Bell, slapped me on the back and announced that he had a story for me. He reminded me that he had been a witness in a juvenile case I had heard a few years before. Let me pass it on to you just as Bob related it to all of us sitting around the table at Whitey's that morning. I hope I do him justice!

"My favorite story involves Gil and me in Juvenile Court. It was about two little kids who broke into Rose's Ice Company and several other places. The last place they entered was the lot where we kept a lot of telephone company trucks parked in stalls.

"These two kids got some trucks cranked up, tried to drive 'em, and tore up about five in the lot tryin' to get one out. They did get one out, finally, by drivin' it right on through the locked gate.

"An officer from the sheriff's department called me about four o'clock in the morning and said, 'Does Southern Bell have a truck number so-and-so assigned to you?'

"I told him, 'Yeah.'

"Then he said, 'We got it out here at the New Hanover County Airport turned over in a ditch.'

"So I went out there, and sure enough, it was upside down in the ditch. They caught the kids, two of them, shortly after that. One little ole boy didn't look like he was over three or four feet tall! He wasn't hardly big enough to ride a tricycle!

"I got a summons to go to court as a witness for the company, and Gil happened to be trying the cases. They had these kids on about 24 different counts, I think. My case was about 18th on the list. Of course, all of them were amusing, but when they got around to mine, I was sittin' there listenin' to Gil and the little ole boys comin' clean on everything. They admitted the whole thing.

"One of the boys, the smaller one, was on the witness stand testifyin'. After he finished, Gil asked him, 'What were you boys doin' out at the airport in a telephone truck?'

"The boy answered, 'Oh, we were gonna steal an

airplane.'

"Gil asked, 'You know how to fly an airplane?'

"The little fellow said, 'Oh, no sir, but we didn't know how to drive them trucks either, until we stole 'em!' "

I told Bob I was gonna have to put that one in my book!

UH, OH! MIGHT AS WELL STAY MARRIED!

This next story has been circulating for years around the New Hanover County Courthouse. I heard it when I came on the bench. By then, procedures had changed regarding the disposition of divorce cases. But years ago in North Carolina, to get an uncontested divorce on the grounds of two years' separation, court protocol dictated a jury trial.

The whole process was pretty straightforward and uncomplicated. Once the judge had instructed the twelve members of the jury, they went out very briefly to deliberate. There really wasn't anything to deliberate since the divorce was uncontested, but they did it anyway. It only took a few minutes, then the twelve jurors returned, answered the standard questions, and the divorce was granted.

Sometimes jury pools would be depleted for one reason or another, and a bailiff would routinely gather up whoever he could find out on the street to round out the twelve needed to hear the divorce case. It was a casual process to say the least, but protocol was -- well, protocol.

I was told that for one particular divorce case, the jury pool had been completely depleted. Twelve jurors had to be quickly rounded up. That day was freezing cold when the bailiff headed outside to offer some volunteers a chance to do their civic duty and maybe get warmed up in the process. Not one did he find. Upon coming back inside however, he noticed that there were plenty of lawyers milling about the courtroom and the corridors, so twelve were recruited to serve on what should have been the briefest of jury experiences.

Testimony was heard, and the judge instructed his degreed jurors, whereupon they retired to the jury room to deliberate. Then the judge took a quick five minute break, fully expecting them to be waiting for him when he returned to the bench. They weren't. The jury box was empty.

Almost a full hour passed, and the judge couldn't imagine why in the world the jurors hadn't returned. So he directed the bailiff to bring them back into court.

When the twelve lawyers had all filed in and were seated, he asked, "Can you tell me if you are close to a decision?"

They all looked at each other somewhat sheepishly before one lawyer stood up and confessed, "Your Honor, we haven't even elected a foreman yet!"

GRANDILOQUENT EXIT

A young man with a cherubic face and a bad attitude pleaded not guilty to a minor traffic offense. Accompanying him to court was his grandmother, from whom he had apparently inherited his disposition. She informed the judge in no uncertain terms that her little angel could not possibly be guilty because he had told her he wasn't. Hard of hearing, she then plunked herself down on the end of a bench just behind her grandson. Cupping both of her hands to her ears, she listened as witnesses' overwhelming testimonies clearly proved her grandson to be guilty.

Together, they glared defiantly at the judge when he pronounced the boy guilty and levied a fine on him. This really upset Grandma's little angel, and he turned and stormed out of the courtroom.

It upset Grandma, too. She angrily jumped up to follow him out, but her wrap-around skirt had come untied, and it sagged to the floor causing a temporary hesitation in her planned march out the back door. From the waist up, she was all business. From the waist down, she was all white slip.

Fueled by anger directed toward the judge, she recovered very quickly. Bending over and snatching the skirt off the floor, she tossed the judge one final glare. Then, mustering all the dignity she could, Grandma stuck her nose up in the air, turned, and marched out of the courtroom trailing her skirt behind.

THE CHARGES WERE DROPPED . . . .

A young woman in her twenties charged her boyfriend with "assault on a female." A trial date was set, and she assured LeAnne Merritt, the assistant district attorney, that she would testify against her boyfriend who had beaten her up. The case came up; the DA was ready; the boyfriend was brought into the courtroom; and you guessed it -- the girlfriend refused to testify. The two lovebirds had made up, and the woman wanted the charges dropped, claiming "nothing happened."

Exasperated, Ms. Merritt reminded her of the beating she said she had suffered. She pointed out that the girlfriend's bruised face disputed her claim that "nothing happened." But the young woman stuck to her story.

The DA explained the circumstances to the judge who said, "Well, if she really refuses to testify, then why not let her drop the charges so we can move on to other cases?"

Still very annoyed, the frustrated assistant district attorney turned to her reluctant witness, and shoved the case file into her hands.

"Here, you can have it!" she retorted.

The black-and-blue faced girlfriend took that file, and did exactly what the judge had suggested. She "dropped the charges" right on the floor, and walked out of the courtroom!

RELUCTANT FARMER

A heavy-set young man with long, dirty brown hair was brought into court charged with larceny. He had a prior record as long as his hair. This time, he was found guilty of stealing a trowel designed to spread and smooth cement.

Before pronouncing his sentence, the judge hearing the case asked, "Why did you steal that trowel?"

"Judge, I was gonna learn how to lay bricks," he replied. "That's sumthin I always wanted to do."

"Oh, really?" the judge replied. "Well let me ask you this. What do you know about farming?"

"Farming?" the defendant asked with a puzzled look on his face. "I don't know nothin' bout farming."

"In that case, I'm going to give you an opportunity to learn a little bit about farming first."

Then he ordered that the thief be confined to the county prison farm for thirty days.

I DEMAND AN ARREST!

A rather well-to-do UNC-Wilmington graduate decided to buy a house for his son to live in while the boy pursued his college education here at his father's alma mater. The father figured that any purchase held for four years would be an excellent investment. So a house in a beautiful, wooded, residential neighborhood was purchased, and his son and two roommates moved in. Then the trouble started.

The son began celebrating his newfound freedom every week-end by hosting a party in his new home. None of the neighbors were invited. None of the neighbors wanted to go. All of the neighbors wanted *him and his roommates* to go -- away, far away.

Cars scattered everywhere, beer cans spilled over into neighbors' yards, and hard rock blasted from the house, shaking the windows of houses unfortunate enough to be within two blocks. Even the trees shuttered.

Calls went out to the police on a regular basis. But every time they responded to a neighbor's plea for relief, their arrival was met with dead silence. The boys just could not be caught. The neighbors suspected that the boys must have had a police scanner, and assigned a "party scanner-man" to monitor it during party time.

This drove one next-door neighbor, a retired gentleman, bonkers. Early one Sunday morning in mid-October, he called the police twice. As usual, their arrivals were met with silence. The neighbor would not take "no" for an answer when the police once again explained that they could not make an arrest, because the students were not breaking the law at that time.

The normally sedate gentleman flew into a rage, and the officer cautioned him to calm down, warning, "You need to be quieter, or I will have to arrest *you!*"

That did it. The poor guy had reached the end of his proverbial rope! He did not calm down, and he was arrested instead of his noisy neighbor.

Following the gentleman's appearance before me in court to answer the charge of "disorderly conduct," I had the student's father contacted. He and I chatted briefly by phone. Apparently, some changes took place because I heard nothing further about problems in that particular neighborhood.

Oh, by the way, I found the neighbor "not guilty."

FREDDIE THE BANKROLLED BOOZER

Freddie was one of my courtroom "regulars." Most district courts that dispose of the bulk of the criminal and traffic cases in their areas have their Freddies, too, I suspect. These are the heavy drinkers who commit petty crimes and parade in and out of court on a regular basis.

You get to know them. They get to know you. Many of them consider the judge to be their friend. Apparently, I had been so honored by Freddie, even though I gave him jail time which interrupted his drinking.

Very tall and slender, Freddie always represented himself. I don't believe he ever hired an attorney, because he seemed to enjoy making the arguments to the judge and the jury. I think he considered that to be his job, and understood that I was just doing mine when I sentenced him. Occasionally Freddie would appeal my decision. But if he chose not to appeal, he always accepted whatever punishment was meted out gracefully, served his time, and then went right back out on the streets and started drinking again.

Back when being drunk in public was a crime in

North Carolina, Freddie developed a criminal record as long as his long, skinny arm. He was always drunk, but never broke. If the particular sentence he had incurred required a fine, he never failed to produce a wad of bills to pay it, along with the court costs. If his sentence was not suspended, then he would peel off enough bills to put up an appeal bond to go to a higher court. The word I heard was that Freddie's family was wealthy, and continually bankrolled their "black sheep" son in order to guarantee his absence from their lives.

One day Freddie spotted me in the hall behind the courtroom and asked, "Judge, do you remember my last case a couple of months ago, when you found me guilty?"

"Certainly, Freddie. I remember it."

"Well," he grinned, "I appealed your decision, and the jury in the higher court decided you were wrong. They found me not guilty!"

I said, "Freddie, now maybe that jury was wrong!" We both chuckled, and he bid me a good-natured farewell.

That was the last I saw of him for a long time. Winter gripped New Hanover County that year in an unrelenting, frigid embrace that claimed the life of one of our other regulars. An old homeless man froze to death beneath a large bush in Greenfield Park. We lost two of our other regulars that winter as well. One fell into the Cape Fear River and drowned. Another burned to death when he fell into a deep, liquor-induced sleep after lighting a fire in an abandoned shed to keep warm.

Freddie's absence did not go unrecognized. Nobody saw him. We all began to worry about him, and feared that something bad had happened to him. One of the bailiff's even commented about his absence. Freddie was still a no-show when winter finally departed, and we all greeted the arrival of Spring with relief. It appeared that our favorite alcoholic had simply disappeared.

One sunny Wednesday morning in late April, I arrived at the courthouse to find long-lost Freddie planted next to my chamber's door. I was pleasantly surprised and somewhat relieved. He was dressed in what once had been an expensive white linen suit. Now it was filthy and looked like he'd slept in it for months. Nevertheless, I was glad to see him.

"Freddie! Where in the world have you been over the past few months?"

Grinning from ear to ear, he looked down at me

and said, "Judge Burnett, I spent the winter in southern Florida. And you know what?"

"What, Freddie?"

"I didn't need a single judge, the entire time I was there!"

Laughing, I said, "Great! I'm glad to hear it!"

That was the last time I ever saw Freddie. I still wonder to this day whatever happened to him. And I have always hoped that wherever he is, he has never "needed" another judge.

SEA MONKEY

Sometimes people who work around boat yards acquire nicknames based on their particular skills. One of my favorite such people was a slender old man who could scurry up a mast in nothing flat. His speed and agility gave him the nickname "Sea Monkey."

To know him was to like him. Sea Monkey befriended an old sea captain, whose boats he worked on over the years at a local boat yard. When the old captain died, some of his family members started squabbling over his will. Greed drove them to contest his decisions on distributions, contending that the old man was senile and incompetent when he signed his will.

Since Sea Monkey knew the old captain quite well, he was called as a witness when the case was heard. On the stand he was asked to state his name for the court.

"My name is Waldo James Moore, Jr.," he revealed. That was the first time a lot of people who were in court, and recognized him, had ever heard his real name.

Question: "Were you friends with the deceased?"

"Yes, sir. I was friends with him all my life."

Question: "Tell the court just about how long that would have been."

"Well, I'm seventy-five years old now, so I'd say for about seventy-five years, then."

Question: "Tell us, how well did you know him?"

"We was real close," Sea Monkey stated firmly.

Question: "Did you notice that right towards the end of his life that the captain had begun talking to himself when he was alone?"

Sea Monkey scratched his head and thought a minute before replying, "Well, Judge, I don't reckon I was ever with him when he was by hisself!"

One time Sea Monkey traded some legal work with Mr. Flynn, a local attorney, for work on the lawyer's boat. Since he got to know Sea Monkey well, Mr. Flynn decided to invite him to the Shriner's annual fish fry.

They both sat down on each side of the corner of a long table to enjoy the fish fillets that were being passed around. When the platter of fish reached Sea Monkey, there were only two fillets of fish left. Sea Monkey sized up the two choices, and immediately helped himself to the best piece, leaving the much smaller, drier fish for Mr. Flynn.

Mr. Flynn decided to have a little fun with his good-natured guest, and teach him some table manners. "Sea Monkey, we need to go over proper etiquette at a dining table," the lawyer announced with a grin.

"Oh, yeah? What's that?" Sea Monkey asked in-between bites.

"Well," Mr. Flynn continued, "when there are two pieces of fish on a plate, one nice one and one not so nice, the proper thing to do is leave the nice one for the next person."

Sea Monkey thought about this for a minute. Then he asked Mr. Flynn, "If the two pieces had come to you first, which one would you have taken?"

"Why, I would have taken the smaller one, of course."

"Well, Mr. Flynn," Sea Monkey noted with a chuckle, "that's the one you got, so what're you fussin' about?"

Yep, he was a favorite. Hardly anybody knew who Waldo James Moore, Jr., was. But we all knew "Sea Monkey."

DISCRIMINATING DEFENDANT

A male witness took the stand to testify in court in an assault case against a female defendant. He explained how abusive her language was toward him and his family. Getting really worked up, he recalled how she had called all of them vulgar, filthy names over and over.

"Judge, she was mad and hollerin' at me, and she changed my name and changed my family's name several times!" he noted with righteous indignation. "She renamed me again and again. Why, she called me every name in the book but the child of God!"

THE SPECIALIST

A case was called one day, and the defendant wasn't present. A brief discussion ensued between the lawyers and the judge as to how to proceed. Suddenly, the defendant, a pleasant looking man in a gray suit, rushed into the courtroom breathing heavily and apologizing profusely for being late.

After being severely reprimanded by the judge for holding up court, the defendant explained, "Your Honor, I'm sorry I'm late. I really am. But you see, I had to go to the tooth doctor."

Maybe the tooth fairy sent him. . . .

FOWL PLAY

In a mountainous section of North Carolina, a wiry little man stood in a courtroom accused of stealing chickens. He entered a plea of "not guilty."

The owner of the chickens was a tough old bird, herself. (Sorry, I couldn't resist!) She insisted that she saw the man steal her chickens, and demanded that he be prosecuted.

The defendant's lawyer kept cross-examining the owner of the birds, trying to create some reasonable doubt in the minds of the jury, hoping to get his client off. Things heated up as the lady got madder and madder at this lawyer. She argued, "Lordy mercy, I saw the thief with the chickens in his hands!"

Much to the surprise of everyone in the courtroom, the defendant was so caught up in the lady's testimony, that he jumped up and shouted out, "You couldn't 'ave seed 'em, 'cause I had 'em hid under my coat!"

MOVIE MISCREANTS

One time I had just finished a case, and was busy making notes at the bench when the district attorney called the defendant in the next case. The "oohs" and "ahhs" that accompanied the defendant down the center aisle of the courtroom made me look up to see who in the world it was. A very handsome, tall, tanned young man with long blond hair smiled acknowledgment of the ladies' response to his entry. He thoroughly enjoyed the effect he was having on the women in the courtroom.

Apparently he was an aspiring actor from California who was in Wilmington working on a film out at the movie studio on N. 23rd Street. North Carolina ranks third in the nation in movie making, and most of the films made in North Carolina are produced in the Wilmington area. I have had the pleasure of meeting many of the bright, talented people in the film industry who flew into our fair city to work on a project. With very few exceptions, they were all hard working, honorable people who are assets to their profession. Having said that, now let me continue with the case of one of those exceptions. . . .

While here in Wilmington, this man had engaged in activities other than film making. He had been charged with one count of larceny, and waived his right to an attorney.

"How do you plead to the charges?" I asked.

"Guilty, Your Honor," he responded without hesitating.

This so-called actor had been caught in the act (pun intended!) of stealing several items, just to see if he could get away with it. He couldn't and he didn't.

"Where are you from?" I asked.

"Californiaaaaaa," he responded dramatically as he looked around at his new-found fans seated in the courtroom.

"Have you been out there very long?"

"No, Your Honor, I haven't."

"Where do you work?"

"I work out in Burbank at a studioooo."

He seemed to enjoy his affected responses to my questions very much, and kept glancing at the ladies to make sure they enjoyed him. I figured it was time for a reality check.

"How long have you been a thief?" I wanted to know.

That got his attention. "I'm not a thief!" he

blurted out indignantly.

"Well, you admit stealing. Isn't that what thieves do?" I pointed out.

Now looking embarrassed, he mumbled, "I don't think of myself as a thief!"

"Well, young man, I do, because *you are.* Furthermore, I am told by this probation officer standing right over here that you're already on probation for another case of larceny. So you're going to do some time, and maybe you'll think about just exactly what you want to be when you get out."

In another case, a minor speeding offense caused a movie producer to appear before me. He, too, was from California, and pled "guilty." While the judgment was being written, I casually asked, "Why didn't you keep an eye on your speedometer?"

"We disconnect them, Your Honor," he replied in a very matter-of-fact tone.

"What do you mean you disconnect them? Why?"

"Well," he patiently explained with a shrug, "we rent cars from Atlanta, and we pay by the mile. So, we disconnect the speedometers. It saves us money."

That blew my mind. After the case had been

resolved, I called up a bailiff. "I want you to find out who the auto leasing company in Atlanta is, and inform them of what's going on with their cars." No more "frequent-driver miles" club perks for Mr. Producer.

I remember one other case involving an actor here for a small part in a television series. He entered a plea of "guilty" to a DWI charge, and refused the assistance of an attorney.

"Where did you do your drinking?" I asked.

"Judge, I drank beer after work at the studio."

"You mean they sell beer at the movie studio?"

"Oh, no, Your Honor, the beer is free!" he assured me.

"So, you mean you work long hours out there, probably don't eat, and then get served enough beer to make you drunk before you get in your car and drive off?"

"That's about right, Sir. You can drink all you want," he admitted.

Later that day, I decided to call the studio's lawyer to make him aware of the potential liability for the movie studio. He appreciated the call very much, and assured me that he would alert the unsuspecting studio executives immediately.

Some digging revealed that a beer distributor had generously provided a huge shipment of a particular brand name of beer to the studio as partial thanks for prominently displaying their can in one scene of a movie. So the freebie beer was being consumed at a record pace.

Apparently, a new policy was enacted after my phone call to the studio lawyer. Instead of drink and then drive, it became drive and then drink. The beer was distributed to employees with the understanding that it would be consumed after they got home, and not beforehand at the studio.

I never had another DWI that involved anyone from the studio out on N. 23rd Street. Maybe it worked. Good.

DON'T RUSH ME

Judge Leonard VanNoppen was holding court up in the Blue Ridge Mountains of North Carolina. Taking a walk outside the courthouse during a lunchtime break, he encountered a nice old gentleman, and started up a conversation.

"Beautiful day out here, isn't it?" Judge VanNoppen said.

"I reckon it is just that," the old man acknowledged.

"You live around here?" the judge asked conversationally.

"Yes, sir, I do."

"Have you lived here all your life?"

The old man drew himself up, looked Judge VanNoppen squarely in the eye and replied firmly, "Well, not yet!"

THE HAYMAKING HITCHHIKER

John J. Burney, Jr., an attorney who practices law in Wilmington, told me this story about his father, who was a Superior Court judge. I enjoyed hearing it, and I'd like to share it with you.

Judge John J. Burney used to ride the circuit throughout eastern North Carolina hearing cases. He was a highly respected judge, known for his unwavering fairness, knowledge of the law, and a terrific sense of humor.

On one occasion, he had to drive to Rocky Mount for the beginning of a jury session of Superior Court. Along the way, he picked up a hitchhiker just outside of town. By coincidence, Judge Burney and his male passenger were both headed for the same trial, but the hitchhiker didn't know that. And he certainly didn't know the judge.

"Where you headed?" Judge Burney asked the young man.

"I've got to go to the courthouse," he explained. "I been tapped for jury duty, but I'm gonna get out of it."

"Really? Why is that?"

"Don't want to do it. I've never served on a jury when I've been called, and I don't plan to start now," the hitchhiker declared.

"How are you going to get out of serving?" the judge wondered.

"Oh, it's easy," the young man assured him. "I always tell the judge I've got to put up hay. It's always got me outta jury duty before, and I plan to tell the judge that today. Works every time."

Judge Burney smiled as he listened. He offered to drop the young hitchhiker off right in front of the courthouse.

"Thanks for the ride. Hope I didn't put you out none," the young man said as he hopped out of the judge's car.

"Good luck inside," called out Judge Burney as his passenger departed.

"No problem!" the young man assured him with a wave.

Then the judge drove around to the back of the courthouse, parked, and went inside to get ready to open court. "I'm going to enjoy this," he said to himself when he entered the courtroom and formally opened the session.

And sure enough, he did! His hitchhiking

passenger turned crimson when they spotted each other. Addressing the jury pool while looking directly at the young man, who was seated in the front row, Judge Burney asked, "Is there anyone who needs to be excused?"

A man and a woman requested and received permission to be excused.

"Anybody else?" the judge asked again.

Silence.

"Anybody here need to put up hay?"

Silence. His hitchhiking companion served all week.

MS. DEMEANOR

One night a policeman stopped a thirty-year-old woman, whose erratic driving caused him to suspect she was drunk. When he pulled her over and approached her car, he discovered a very attractive woman displaying a lot of cleavage in a low-cut blouse.

Struggling to stay focused on the task, he escorted her to the police station's breathalyzer room so that he could give her a breath test to determine what her blood alcohol level was. The woman tried very hard to conduct herself with great dignity, which belied her somewhat suggestive attire. Meanwhile, the poor officer kept silently reminding himself to "stay focused on the task."

After reading the woman her rights, the officer set up the machine, and turned to explain, "Now I have to check your breasts . . . . *breath*, I mean *breath*! *Breath*! I have to check your breath!" His face flushed bright red.

As the woman prepared to blow into the breathalyzer, she inhaled deeply. Her bosom strained against the buttons of her blouse, threatening to send them flying across the room.

It was a rough night for the officer.

FORGET STICKS AND STONES

Judge Leonard VanNoppen heard that Harry, a heavy drinker, and one of his most frequent "regulars" in court, had been bad-mouthing him. One day during one of his lunch breaks, Leonard spotted Harry on a street corner near the courthouse. Harry and some of his cronies were doing what Harry did best -- drinking cheap booze.

Just for the hell of it, the judge walked over and decided to confront Harry about his critical remarks. "Did you tell my buddy Bill Sizemore that I'm a damn rascal?"

Harry gazed up at Judge VanNoppen through an alcoholic fog and slowly responded, "Naw, I didn't tell him no sech thang. I don't know how he found out!"

TIPPED OFF

While in Raleigh for a conference, I decided to go across the street from my hotel to an all-night diner late one night when hunger took precedence over my need to sleep. The place was about empty.

I seated myself on a stool at the counter just as one man was finishing up. He left a dime and a quarter under the edge of his plate as a tip. Before his dishes could be cleared by the waitress, another guy came in, sat down next to the dirty dishes, and swiped the tip. Realizing that I'd spotted him doing it, he winked and moved two stools away. I figured he knew the waitress and was going to kid around with her.

I waited. The waitress, a very courteous lady named Betsy, came and took my order and then cleared away the dirty dishes. I looked at the man again, and he put his finger to his mouth, and went "Shhhhhhhhh."

When I finished eating, I decided to give the guy one more chance. I said, "Hey, buddy, if you don't give the waitress the tip you swiped, I'll tell her you took it."

Again, he shushed me. So I called Betsy over, who called the manager over, who confronted the man, who denied everything.

At that point, I said, "Look, I saw you steal her tip! If they take you to court, I'll drive back up here to Raleigh and testify against you."

This time he didn't shush me up. Instead, he jumped up and pulled the two coins out of his right pant's pocket and threw them against the wall behind the counter. Then he ran out of the building.

The waitress thanked me, and we all considered the case closed. No, I didn't forget to leave her a tip!

WISH GRANTED

One of the "perks" of attending judges' conferences was knowing that I'd always return to New Hanover County with another anecdote or two for my growing collection of stories. Here's one I heard at just such a conference not long before I retired.

A seemingly healthy young man kept trying to check himself into the local hospital of a town in the northern part of our state for no apparent reason. The security guards kept escorting him out, and he just kept coming right back. Finally, the hospital's chief of security lost his patience with the man, and had him arrested for loitering.

When he was brought into court for his first appearance, the judge asked, "Young man, why do you keep going back to the hospital?"

"Your Honor, I'm pregnant," he declared with a seriousness that warranted a phone call.

That phone call was made to Mental Health, and the poor guy finally got his wish. With a little help and an escort, he checked into the hospital. And this time, he wasn't asked to leave for quite a while.

SMITE NOT!

One day a young man, acting terribly upset, appeared before me in court. His girlfriend had sworn out a warrant against him for assaulting her. I first thought that his agitation was self-directed for the abuse he had allegedly caused the young lady, who was also present.

But I found out otherwise when their case was called. To expedite matters, I suggested that they be sworn in simultaneously. They both came forward from opposite sides of the courtroom. The accused moved slowly, and appeared to be extremely nervous. He stood shifting his weight from one foot to the other, and hesitated when he was instructed to place his right hand on the Bible by the bailiff.

"What's the problem?" I asked.

"Judge," he explained as his eyes darted from his girlfriend to me, "I don't wanna take a chance on touchin' that woman! Can I use a separate Bible?"

His request was granted.

HIS SIXTH SENSE

A self-proclaimed "Lover Boy" enjoyed the attention of two attractive young ladies right up until the night that one of them caught him with the other one.

Using the key that LB had so generously provided, one of the ladies let herself into his apartment one night to surprise him. She did. LB was buck-naked and in the midst of vigorously entertaining the other young lady.

It turned out that LB didn't like surprises. So he tried to force his uninvited guest to leave. But she wasn't quite ready to go. First, she tore into LB while the other young lady called the police. Then that lady joined forces with the intruder; and together, they really let him have it. It was not a pretty sight. But guess who wound up being charged with assault? Yep, ole Lover Boy himself!

Still befuddled and dumbfounded when he was hauled into court, LB stood before the judge with lingering traces of bruises and scratches. Greatly chagrined, he declared, "Judge, I ain't never gonna git in a mess like this agin! I'll think things through. I swear I'm gonna use my condom sense next time!"

SOBRIETY PROPRIETY

A homeless man in one of North Carolina's largest cities, charged with being drunk and disruptive, was due in court on a particular day. He arrived late, and sat down on the back row of the courtroom quite drunk and once again, disruptive.

At first, he just started mumbling quietly to no one in particular. But the longer he sat, the louder he jabbered. Finally, Judge Sandra Levi ordered a bailiff to bring the man up to the bench. Very annoyed by his disruption, she scolded him and let him know in no uncertain terms that he was not to drink in her courtroom.

He stood before her weaving from side to side, and insisted, "Judge, I weren't drinkin' in your court."

Incensed, Judge Levi repeated, "You will not be in my court drinking! Do you understand?"

Weaving as he held onto the bench, the old guy earnestly assured her, "Yur Honor, I ain't drinkin' in court! I quit drinkin' jus 'fore I cum in the door."

HARD HEADED

One night in mid-December, two local men we'll call Bobby and Roy, were arrested and charged with armed robbery of a couple on a downtown Wilmington street. When asked how they pled in court to the charge, they both steadfastly maintained their innocence, and each firmly responded, "not guilty."

Bobby testified that they were not even in the area at the time of the alleged robbery, while Roy declared that furthermore, they also had an alibi. However, an eyewitness to the robbery easily identified Roy, because he didn't wear a mask, unlike his partner in crime, who did. And a jailhouse "snitch," who briefly shared a cell with both of them, testified that he had heard Bobby talk about doing the deal, but said Bobby wasn't worried about being caught because he did wear a mask.

After a knockdown, drag-out fight in court, the jury found Roy guilty, and Bobby not guilty. As the bailiff prepared to escort Roy back to jail, Bobby wasted no time heading in the opposite direction. But just before they both disappeared through doors at opposing ends of the courtroom, Bobby couldn't resist turning around toward Roy and calling out, "I told you, man. You shoulda wore a mask!"

THE LAST WORD

After a long night of hard drinking, the owner of a Harley-Davidson bike staggered out of a bar on Front Street, and spotted a Honda bike parked next to his. In front of some other late night boozers, he kicked it over and then urinated on it before climbing on his own bike and weaving off. Furious, the Honda owner hauled him into court for damages. The offending biker pleaded "guilty," and the case was quickly concluded.

As the defendant walked away from the bench, I noticed a blonde-headed brunette in a tight, black leather mini skirt preparing to depart with him. I recognized her as someone who had come into court quite a few times, accompanying various people. I sorta felt like I knew her, and just for the hell of it, I motioned for her to come to the bench.

Knowing what the answer would be ahead of time, I nevertheless asked, "Why did your friend kick over the bike and urinate on it?"

"Judge," she said, "it was a *Japanese* bike!"

Again, anticipating her answer, I innocently asked, "What difference does that make?"

Exasperated, she put her hands on her hips and

responded, "Judge, we were in a war with the Japanese!"

Knowing that the biker was too young to have been in the military during World War II, I still couldn't resist asking, "Was your friend in the war?"

"No."

Enjoying myself, I continued, "I was a pilot in the Army Air Corps (now the US Air Force) during the war, and I don't kick over Hondas."

She paused a moment, smiled, and moved a little closer to the bench. "Well now, Judge, maybe you just ought to consider it," she replied softly.

Then she slowly turned around, sashayed up the center aisle and disappeared out the courtroom door without a backward glance.

NO DUMMY

At Whitey's Restaurant early one morning, Charlie "Bubba" Deluka strolled in, spotted me, and made his way over to my table. "Hey, Judge," he announced, "I got a story for your book."

Bubba is a law enforcement officer with a lot of experience. Over the years, he has run into all sorts of offenders. On this particular morning, after placing his breakfast order and fixing his cup of coffee, he proceeded to tell me about this one guy who really tried his patience.

Bubba had been on routine patrol a couple of nights before, and had noticed an old Chevrolet weaving back and forth across the road. Stopping the car, he discovered a male driver about sixty years old, about six-foot-six, about 250 pounds, and about as drunk as he'd ever seen. He charged the man with a DWI. The man was so drunk that he couldn't understand much of anything that Bubba told him to do. Three gold upper teeth protruded from his mouth as he just sat in his car grinning and nodding.

Finally, Bubba said he managed to get the big guy to the sheriff department's breathalyzer room.

There he sat him down, advised him of his rights, and instructed the man to put the breathalyzer mouthpiece in his mouth.

"Now, mister, I want you to blow on this."

The man fumbled with the mouthpiece, put it in his mouth and then spit it right out. Still smiling. Lots of gold.

"Do it again," Bubba said. "Put it in your mouth and blow through it."

The man sniffed it.

Bubba tried again. "Look, I want you to put this piece here in your mouth, and blow on it. Okay?"

No luck. Bubba said it went on for quite a while. Bubba said he was losing his patience. "Look, man, do you see that damn green light right there? Do you see it?"

Bubba said he had raised his voice.

"Yeah," the drunk grinned up at him, flashing gold.

"Well, you blow on that thing until you see that green light go out! Do it! Now!"

Bubba said he had lost his patience.

At that point, the hefty drunk had apparently lost his, too. He looked up at Bubba like he was an idiot. "Are you nuts? You think I'm crazy as hell? I got 'nuf sense to know I ain't gonna blow out no 'lectric light!"

Bubba said he came close to turning the man loose.

JUST A FIGUREHEAD

Judge Phil Ginn used to hold court high up in the Great Smoky Mountains of North Carolina. Just like me, he had his "regulars" who appeared before him all the time for one thing or another. One of them was a grizzled old man who went by the name of Colonel Bingham. Phil told me the colonel never could stay sober for very long, and had been in court so many times, he never bothered getting himself an attorney. He simply preferred to represent himself.

So it was no surprise to Phil when Colonel Bingham appeared before him on charges of drunk and disorderly conduct one early August morning. And it was no surprise that the colonel pleaded guilty. He always did, because he always was.

Phil said on this particular occasion, he decided to ask about the origin of the old man's title. "Colonel Bingham, before you go, I want to ask you something."

"What's that, yer Honor?"

"What does the 'Colonel' before your name mean? Were you in the military?"

"Aw, no, Judge. It's like the 'Judge' 'fore your name. It don't mean nothin'."

CAP'N TOM

For many years in New Hanover County, the court has allowed persons convicted of minor offenses to do community work in lieu of doing straight time in prison. Many of those convicted picked up trash alongside our roadways.

On one occasion, "Keep America Beautiful" wanted to publicize the work program, and enlisted my help. I agreed to pick up trash on the side of a very littered road for the benefit of the television cameras. On the appointed morning, I started filling up a plastic bag before the TV crew arrived, but not before a man I'd sentenced in court several times rode up on his bicycle. Wearing jeans, a T-shirt, and a baseball cap with the name "TOM" emblazoned on it, he paused and spoke to me.

"Hey, Judge Burnett, what in the world are you doin' out here?"

I explained the "Keep America Beautiful" promotion. Then he said, "Judge, you've convicted me in court several times. Do you remember my name?"

I stood up, dropped my bag on the ground, and glanced at his cap. "Sure do, Tom. Of course I remember you."

Looking rather surprised, he shook his head in amazement as he hopped back on his bike. "Man that's really somethin'!" he muttered to himself as he rode off. "I can't believe he remembered my name."

He glanced back at me once, and I just waved and smiled, "Bye, Tom!"

TAKE HER, PLEASE!

One afternoon I was leaving the courthouse when I heard someone calling me. I turned around to discover a very nice looking middle-aged lady, and an equally attractive younger lady hurrying toward me.

"Judge, will you marry my daughter?" the older of the two asked.

I knew she was confusing me with the magistrates who, unlike judges, actually do perform marriages in North Carolina. Nevertheless, unable to resist, I replied, "Your daughter is beautiful, and I'm sure she'd make a great wife, but I'm already married."

The mother turned beet red, and stammered, "Oh, I didn't mean . . . . that is, I mean . . . ."

I chuckled, and quickly said, "I'm kidding. I know what you mean. I'm just exercisin' a little judicial humor!"

Relieved, the mother laughed. Her daughter smiled. And I directed them to the Magistrate's office.

UPSTAGED BY A STOGIE

Years ago, smoking was allowed in court. One particular attorney, we'll call him Stephen Henry, perfected a way to use cigars to help him win his cases in court. This is the story of just exactly how he managed to accomplish that, as it was told to me.

When the opposing attorney rose to address the jurors with his closing argument, Stephen Henry would light up a long cigar. The more long-winded the unsuspecting lawyer was, the more it helped Mr. Henry.

Stephen would puff on his cigar, expelling considerable smoke. This got the attention of the jury. While his opponent talked, Stephen Henry never flicked the ashes off. As he continued to smoke his cigar, he would hold it up, roll it around in his fingers, and stare at the ashes. So did the jurors. Fascinated. You could almost hear them inwardly screaming to themselves, *"When are they going to fall off?"* The opposing lawyer might as well have been addressing a collective gathering of tree stumps.

When the hapless attorney concluded his speech to the jury, Stephen would very carefully lay his cigar down so as not to disturb the growing shaft of ashes.

One day a lawyer, who had been upstaged one too many times, figured out what was going on. He discovered that Mr. Henry would secretly stick several long, thin wires into his stogie, which would shore up the ashes as they burned. The end result? Stephen Henry stole the show!

REMEMBER ME?

While on my lunch break one day, I stopped my car at my bank's drive-thru window to make a deposit. While I was waiting, the teller spoke to me over the intercom. "Judge Burnett, there's a man in here who wants to cash a check. When I asked him for some identification, like a driver's license, he said he didn't have one. But . . . ."

I could see the man inside the bank looking at me through the large window from across the counter. Pointing to me, he interrupted the teller and declared indignantly, "I don't have a driver's license. But that judge right out there knows me, because he took mine!"

THE LOL TERROR

A very feisty, little old lady took the witness stand one day. She had brought charges of assault and battery against another elderly lady. As she began to tell her side of the story, she got her dander up.

When the judge asked her to describe what the defendant did to her, she jumped up and slammed her folded umbrella down on the judge's bench. "Judge," she yelled, "that ole coot said 'I'm gonna cut yer ass 'til yer nose bleeds'!"

Startled, the judge directed a bailiff to hold the little lady's umbrella until she had finished testifying, just for safe keeping of course. . . .

SENATOR SAM

I have no more court related stories. I'm just telling you this up front, in case you want to stop reading right now. You see, this last story doesn't "fit in" with all the rest. It's a true story that happened to me before I even graduated from law school. So I can't really justify including it in this book. But my ego overruled my heart and mind, as it admittedly, frequently does. So here it is. I hope, if you're still reading, that you will understand, and enjoy it.

It's about Senator Samuel James Ervin, Jr. I idolized the man. Born up in Morganton, he distinguished himself at several levels of government throughout his career. After graduating from the University of North Carolina at Chapel Hill, he went on to receive his law degree from Harvard Law School in 1922. From then until he died in 1985 at the age of 88, Senator Sam, as he was affectionately known, practiced law, served in the NC general assembly, was a judge on both local and state levels, served briefly as a congressman, and then as a senator for twenty years. To this day -- I modestly submit to you there has never been another senator who has represented the citizens of North Carolina with such integrity and excellence as Senator Sam did. I was so proud to have crossed paths with him. Here's the story of just how that happened.

When I was a senior in law school at the Wake Forest College School of Law, I served as president of the Student Bar Association. The year was 1956, and my class would be the last class to graduate from Wake Forest, while still located in the small town of the same name just north of Raleigh. That summer, the whole school moved west to the big city of Winston-Salem, where in 1967, it was designated a university.

One of my duties as president of the Student Bar Association was to secure a speaker for our annual Law Day, held each Spring for students, faculty and alumni. I was absolutely thrilled when Senator Sam graciously accepted the invitation extended to him to be our banquet's main speaker. And I eagerly looked forward to picking him up at the Raleigh-Durham airport when the appointed day finally arrived.

His flight was scheduled to touch down at 4:00 o'clock in the afternoon, two hours before the festivities back at Wake Forest were to begin. My job was to transport him safely over the approximately twenty-five miles from the airport to the head table where he was to give the main speech. Twenty-five miles -- two hours -- no problem. . . .

Well, actually, I had been having a few problems with my old green, Buick convertible. The top leaked, and the electric windows remained forever halfway opened or closed, depending on whether you're an optimist or a pessimist. Oh yes, and then there was a slight problem with the engine overheating -- whenever I drove it any distance. But, in anticipation of picking up the senator, I had that fixed. And to my great relief, no rain was forecast on the big day. Good. Figured I had everything covered.

Accompanied by my father, John Henry Burnett, himself a graduate of Wake Forest School of Law, and Alex Biggs, a fellow law student, I hit the road. Okay, I admit it. My ego was running wild.

. . . . And my Buick's engine started running hot on the way back from the airport to Wake Forest. I could not believe it. I thought it was fixed! This was definitely not part of the plan! Neither were the ominous black clouds beginning to gather overhead. Suddenly my honored guest, my father, and my buddy were all in danger of getting stranded and soaked at the same time. Not cool. I privately berated myself for not borrowing my father's car, which he had offered.

Choosing the back roads of Wake County (some of which were dirt), in order to avoid Raleigh city traffic, had seemed like a good idea that would help guarantee our prompt arrival at the college. Now I wasn't so sure. Looking desperately right and left for a source of water, I spotted a farmer out standing in his field. I whipped the car off the road, pulled up into his yard, jumped out and charged toward him.

"Sir, my car's overheating. Could you please let me have some water for my radiator?" I explained my dilemma, as he shuffled over to his well, and proceeded to fill a bucket full of water. "We're in a big hurry," I continued. "I've got Senator Sam Ervin in the car, and I have to get him to Wake Forest by 6:00 o'clock, and it looks like it might rain and my car's windows won't shut, and . . . ." I was in immediate danger of losing some of my composure.

The farmer eyed me and my car suspiciously. From across his yard, my Buick's black leather interior coupled with the darkening sky made it impossible to see who was in the car. I guess he figured there was no way that the distinguished senator would be caught dead in a beat-up car like mine. I sensed his unease, and said to myself, "Uh, oh! He probably thinks I'm going to rob him!" That just made me talk even faster. I pleaded, "Senator Ervin really is in the car. I'm taking him to Wake Forest to give a speech. I'm not kidding! He's in the backseat. I'll introduce you to him."

Never taking his eyes off of me, the old farmer slowly backed away from the well, over toward the rear of my car. Then he stooped and peered cautiously into the back seat. "Well I'll be damned!" he shouted. "That really is Senator Ervin!" And as if I didn't feel bad enough already, he added, "Senator, I'm mighty sorry you're havin' all this trouble."

Senator Sam just looked at the farmer with that famous twinkle in his eye, and responded, "Well, it's not so bad. If we hadn't had this trouble, I wouldn't have met you!"

After topping off my radiator, we barely made it back to the campus in time for the banquet. When he rose to speak, Senator Sam pulled out all the stops. He regaled the audience that evening with the tale of his ride from the airport. Everybody loved it. . . . . And quite honestly, so did I.

Almost twenty years later, I was delighted to have the opportunity to hear the senator speak at the

American Bar Association conference I attended in Hawaii. By this time, Senator Sam had played a unique role in history. He had chaired the Senate Select Committee on Presidential Campaign Activities which, in part, investigated the infamous Watergate break-in. As you all know, this eventually led to President Richard Nixon's resignation in 1974.

Wanting so very much for the privilege of saying "hello" once again, I waited patiently after Senator Sam's speech for the throng surrounding him to disburse. As I stood there remembering that long ago trip from the Raleigh-Durham airport to Wake Forest with this, the most powerful and influential person I had ever chauffeured, I wondered if he would remember it, too. When he finally turned toward me, I stepped up, introduced myself and asked, "Senator, do you remember speaking at Wake Forest Law School when I had car trouble?"

He remembered. Boy, did he remember! Without even hesitating, and with that ever present twinkle in his eye, Senator Sam once again treated me to his funny recollection of our trip from the airport back to Wake Forest. Sharing a good old down-home belly laugh together, we shook hands and then parted.

When I walked away from him that day, I felt the

special thrill of having been in the presence of someone quite extraordinary. Yep, I still idolized Senator Sam.

ABOUT THE AUTHOR

Gilbert Henry Burnett never intended to don a black robe and sit in judgment of his peers in a court of law. In fact, he never intended to become a lawyer, either. Instead, Gil arrived at the bench only after taking a somewhat circuitous route through several other occupational choices first.

In June, 1953, a bolt out of the blue -- quite literally -- finally pointed him in the direction of law school. That's when a hosiery mill he owned and operated with a partner in Raleigh was struck by lightening and burned to the ground. Jolted by such a loss, and with a wife and two little girls to support, Gil reevaluated his career choices. That fall, he entered the Wake Forest School of Law, and graduated in 1956.

Gil chose to establish his law practice in Wilmington, close to his home town of Burgaw. In 1968, he ran successfully for District Court judge, and enjoyed an uncontested 23 years on the bench before retiring in 1991 as the Chief District Court Judge for North Carolina's Fifth Judicial District.

Today, the retired judge continues a lifelong tradition of refusing to allow a single blade of grass to grow beneath his busy feet. Divorced, he maintains an energetic schedule of civic-minded activities, travels extensively, and works out three days a week at a local health club. He derives great pleasure in visiting his three children and four grandchildren, and taking friends out for excursions on his sailboat, Sailbad the Sinner.

Rebecca M. Lewis
Wilmington, NC
June, 2000